STEM-gineers

gineers

MASTERS OF MATHS

WAYLAND

First published in paperback in
Great Britain in 2022 by Wayland
Copyright © Hodder and Stoughton, 2018

Wayland
An imprint of Hachette
Children's Group
Part of Hodder & Stoughton
Carmelite House
50 Victoria Embankment
London EC4Y 0DZ

Series editor: Elise Short
Produced by Tall Tree Ltd
Written by: Rob Colson
Designer: Ben Ruocco

ISBN: 978 1 5263 0842 9
10 9 8 7 6 5 4 3 2 1

An Hachette UK Company
www.hachette.co.uk
www.hachettechildrens.co.uk

Printed and bound in Dubai

The website addresses (URLs) included in this book were valid at the time of going to press. However, it is possible that contents or addresses may have changed since the publication of this book. No responsibility for any such changes can be accepted by either the author or the Publisher.

Picture credits
t–top, b–bottom, l–left, r–right, c–centre,
front cover–fc, back cover–bc
All images courtesy of Dreamstime.com and all
icons made by Freepik from www.flaticon.com,
unless indicated:

Inside front danielo/Shutterstock; fc, bc Deviney;
fcr, 24l dgstudio; fccl, Southernstar71; fcbl,
28bl Wolfgang Beyer/Attribution-ShareAlike 3.0
Unported (CC BY-SA 3.0); fccl, 18bl André Hatala;
4bl Maryana Gilevich ; 4-5 Chrisdorney,
5cr Morphart Creation/Shutterstock; 6bl
Marekuliasz; 6cr Szilas; 7tr Arbazbagwanfi;
8cr http://likesuccess.com/author/euclid;
8b Andreykuzmin; 9t Lars H. Rohwedder/GFDL/
Attribution-ShareAlike 3.0 Unported (CC BY-SA
3.0); 9br Bjørn Christian Tørrissen/Attribution-
ShareAlike 3.0 Unported (CC BY-SA 3.0);
10b Andrew Park/Shutterstock; 11b Gonin;
12cl Starserfer; 12b Photka; 13bl NASA;
14cl Tinamou; 15tl Joingate; 15cr Arbazbagwanfi;
17br Peterhermesfurian; 18-19 Gdolgikh;
19tl ann131313/Shutterstock; 19tr Enricolapponi;
19br gagarych/Shutterstock; 19br darvis/
Shutterstock; 20bc Ian Watson; 20-21 Niagara
College; 22-23 Tatiana Popova/Shutterstock;
24l Maxcrepory; 25tl NSA; 26b Elke Wetzig/
Attribution-ShareAlike 3.0 Unported (CC BY-SA
3.0); 26-27 sakhorn/Shutterstock; 29tl Paha_l;
29cl Marilyna; 29r Solkoll.

Every effort has been made to acknowledge every
image source but the publisher apologises for any
unintentional errors or omissions that will be
corrected in future editions of this book.

CONTENTS

MATHEMATICS ALL AROUND US

Mathematics is a powerful tool that allows us to measure the world around us. From simple systems of counting, early mathematicians developed techniques such as arithmetic, algebra and geometry to create calendars, keep trade records or calculate taxes. Today, mathematicians use complex systems to dig into the deepest mysteries of the universe.

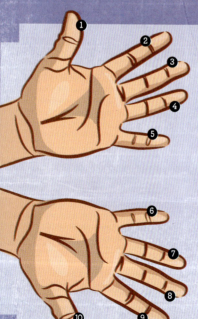

Counting bases

We usually count in a number system known as base 10, or the decimal system, with one digit for each of our fingers and thumbs.

Sometimes we count in bases other than base 10. For example, to count time, we use base 60, or the sexagesimal system, dividing an hour into 60 minutes and a minute into 60 seconds. This system dates back to the ancient Babylonians 4,000 years ago. Base 60 is useful because 60 is the smallest number that can be divided by 2, 3, 4, 5 and 6 (as well as 10, 12, 15, 20 and 30). This makes it easy to divide an hour into equal parts.

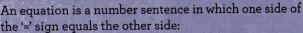

A clock face counts minutes in base 60, and hours in base 12.

Solving equations

An equation is a number sentence in which one side of the '=' sign equals the other side:

$$5 \times 3 = 18 - 3$$

In algebra, some of the numbers in an equation are replaced by a letter. The job of the mathematician is to solve the equation to find the value the letter represents:

$$y + 7 = 2 \times 5 \text{ therefore } y = 3$$

Formulas show the relationship between two quantities, allowing you to substitute different values. For instance, the formula for converting pounds into kilograms is this:

$y = 5\,x\,/\,11$, where y is the weight in kilograms and x is the weight in pounds. '/' means 'divided by'.

Mathematics in Wonderland

By the 19th century, new ideas had been introduced into mathematics that seemed impossible in the real world, such as the square root of -1. English mathematician Lewis Carroll poked fun at many of these ideas in his 1865 novel *Alice's Adventures in Wonderland*. In the book, Alice is transported to a world in which impossible things happen all the time. She tries to remember her times tables, but finds that numbers behave very differently in Wonderland, probably because she is no longer counting in base 10.

Read on to discover the problems that mathematicians have solved through the ages. The answers to questions in the projects are found on page 31.

RIGHT-ANGLED TRIANGLES

All triangles have three internal angles that add up to 180 degrees (°). In a right-angled triangle, one of those angles is always 90°. Right-angled triangles have many special properties that make them extremely useful to mathematicians. The most important property was proved by the mathematician Pythagoras.

Pythagoras (c.570 BCE–c.500 BCE)

The Greek philosopher Pythagoras ran a school in southern Italy. He taught his students that the principles of mathematics provided the key to understanding the universe. The stories we have about his life and teachings have been passed down in the form of legends and myths. It is possible that either he or one of his students first wrote down the proof of his famous theorem.

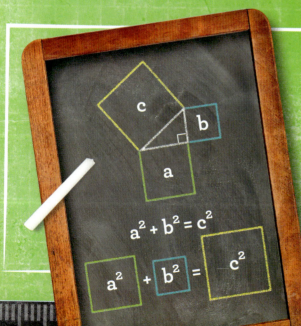

$$a^2 + b^2 = c^2$$

$$a^2 + b^2 = c^2$$

The Pythagorean theorem

The Pythagorean theorem states that: the square of the hypotenuse (the side of a right-angled triangle opposite the right angle – here c) is equal to the sum of the squares of the other two sides (a and b). In other words, when squares are made on each of the three sides, the biggest square has the exact same area as the other two squares put together.

Pythagorean triples

Pythagorean triples are the lengths of the sides of right-angled triangles with whole number values. Examples of Pythagorean triples are:
(3,4,5), (5,12,13), (8,15,17), (7,24,25), (9,40,41)

Each of these triples has different internal angles. Triangles that are different sizes but have the same angles are called similar triangles. You can make similar triangles from the Pythagorean triples by multiplying each side by the same number. For instance, the Pythagorean triples **(6,8,10)** and **(9,12,15)** make similar triangles to **(3,4,5)**.

Calculating heights

Right-angled triangles are used in the branch of mathematics called trigonometry. Knowing the angles of a right-angled triangle and the length of one of the sides allows you to calculate the lengths of the other sides. Surveyors use trigonometry to calculate the heights of buildings, among other things. Using an instrument called a theodolite, they measure the angle to the top of the building from a particular distance away from it.

If you move away from a building to a distance where the theodolite measures 45°, you have created a right-angled triangle with two sides of equal length. You know that the height of the building is your distance from it plus the height of the theodolite above the ground.

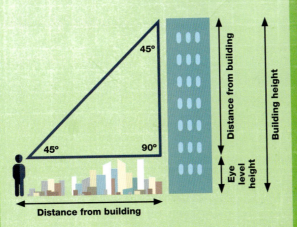

PROJECT:
VISUAL PROOF

There are many ways to prove the Pythagorean theorem. Pythagoras himself is said to have used this visual proof, which you can recreate.

You will need: a pen, card and a ruler

1. First cut out four identical right-angled triangles.
2. Arrange the triangles in a square with the four right angles at the four corners of the square. Trace the square and cut it out.
3. Inside the square, the triangles form a smaller square with sides the length of the hypotenuse (*c*).
4. Rearrange the triangles so that they form two rectangles within the same square. The spaces left behind are two smaller squares of sides the length of *a* and *b*.

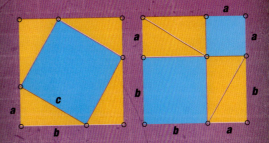

Do you see how this shows that $a^2 + b^2 = c^2$?

SHAPES AND SPACE

Geometry is the field of mathematics that studies the properties of shapes and space. The mathematical structure of space was first worked out by the ancient Greek mathematician Euclid.

Euclid (c.325–265 BCE)

Working in Alexandria in northern Egypt, Euclid set out his ideas in the book *Elements* – one of the oldest maths books in existence. In the book, Euclid uses logic to produce a set of theorems (true statements) that can be worked out from a set of axioms (basic truths). In doing so, he laid the foundations for the study of geometry, which we still use today.

Euclid's axioms

Euclid defined five axioms, or basic truths, that he believed to always hold true in geometry:

1. It is always possible to draw a straight line from one point to another.
2. It is always possible to extend a straight line in a straight line.
3. A circle is described by giving its centre and its radius.
4. All right angles are equal to one another.
5. Given a straight line and a point not lying on the line, there is just one straight line going through the point that is parallel to the line.

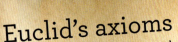

Point A

Only one line exists that passes through point A and is parallel to line B. This is the fifth of Euclid's axioms, known as the parallel postulate.

Parallel lines

Line B

From these basic ideas, many other properties of shapes can be worked out: for instance, that the three internal angles of a triangle always add up to 180°.

Bending space

For thousands of years, Euclid's geometry was thought to be the only geometry possible. In the 19th century, mathematicians such as the great German Carl Friedrich Gauss (1777–1855) worked out forms of geometry in which Euclid's five axioms do not hold true. For instance, the surface of a sphere, such as Earth, is not a Euclidean space. If you draw two lines at right angles to one another from the equator, they will meet at one of the poles, creating a triangle with angles of more than 180°. A triangle drawn on a small section of the sphere will have angles that add up to very nearly 180°.

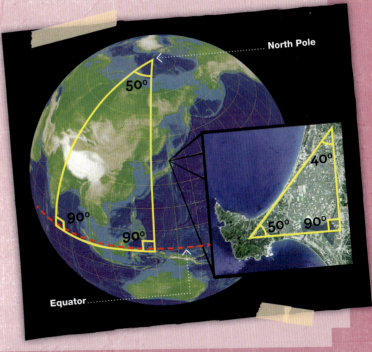

North Pole

50°

90°

90°

40°

50°   90°

Equator

PROJECT:
THE PENROSE TRIANGLE

Many mathematicians play with geometry to draw shapes that would be impossible to make in three dimensions. In the 1950s, British mathematician Roger Penrose described this impossible triangle.

You will need: a pencil, a pair of compasses, a piece of paper, a rubber, a ruler

1. First, draw a single line of any length. Set your compasses to that length and draw two arcs that intersect one another setting the stylus at either end of the line. Draw straight lines to the point of intersection to make an equilateral triangle.
2. Set the compasses to a much smaller circle and draw circles around each corner of the triangle. Extend the lines of the triangle so that they touch the circle and label the points (see right).
3. Draw the following lines:
D to K, L to I, I to F, F to E, L to G, E to B,
D to A, A to B, A to J, J to I, H to C
4. Carefully rub out the other lines to leave this shape:

A   B

C   D

L   G

J   K   H   E

I   F

Can you see how this shape cannot exist in three dimensions?

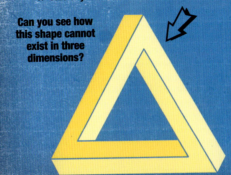

Seen from one angle, this sculpture in Perth, Australia, looks like this.

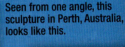

From another angle, it looks like a Penrose triangle!

DEVELOPING NUMBERS

The number line places numbers in order around zero. Positive numbers are placed to the right of zero, while negative numbers are placed to the left. The mathematical rules of the number zero, with positive and negative numbers to either side of it, were first developed in India 1,500 years ago.

-5 -4 -3 -2 -1 0 1 2 3 4 5 6 7 8 9 10

Aryabhata (476–550 CE)

The Indian Aryabhata was the first mathematician to use the idea of zero in his number system. He wrote his great mathematical work the *Aryabhatiya* at the age of just 23. In this book, which is written as a series of poetic verses, Aryabhata describes the place-value notation system that we use today, including the use of zero to show the absence of a value. In place-value notation, each digit represents a power of ten:

Ten thousands	Thousands	Hundreds	Tens	Units		Tenths	Hundredths	Thousandths
10,000	1,000	100	10	1	.	0.1	.01	.001

Starting at zero

Building on the work of Aryabhata, his fellow Indian Brahmagupta (598–668 CE) was the first mathematician to give the rules defining zero, treating it as a number in its own right. Brahmagupta also introduced the idea of negative numbers.

०	0
१	1
२	2
३	3
४	4
५	5
६	6
७	7
८	8
९	9
१०	10

Ancient Indian digits (left) are lined up with their modern equivalents (right).

Rational or irrational

In between the whole numbers on the number line are the fractions, which are written in the form a/b (a divided by b), where a and b are whole numbers. Together with the whole numbers, these form a set of numbers called the rational numbers.

Some numbers cannot be written down in the form of a/b. These are called the irrational numbers, and they include numbers such as the square root of 2: $\sqrt{2}$ ($\sqrt{2} \times \sqrt{2} = 2$). To five decimal places, $\sqrt{2}$ = 1.41421. We can never write down the exact value of an irrational number, meaning that the numbers to the right of the decimal point go on forever, without ever forming a repeating pattern.

Complex numbers

Together, the rational and irrational numbers form a set of numbers called the real numbers. There is also another set of numbers that do not appear on the number line. These are called complex numbers, which include the imaginary number i, defined as the square root of -1. Complex numbers play an important part in physics, such as describing the behaviour of tiny particles.

Complex numbers are also used to code electronic music.

PROJECT: DECIMAL FRACTIONS

Fractions have two parts: the numerator at the top and the denominator at the bottom.

You will need: a pen, piece of paper or notebook

Decimal fractions have a denominator that is a power of 10 (10, 100, 1000, etc), and are often written using a decimal point. For example, $73/100$ = 0.73. You can convert a fraction into a decimal fraction by dividing the numerator by the denominator using long division. For instance, $1/8$ = 0.125. Not all fractions can be converted exactly into decimal fractions. For instance, $5/6$ = 0.8333… ('…' means that the 3s go on for ever).

Can you convert the following fractions into decimal fractions:
a) $2/3$
b) $5/8$
c) $41/40$

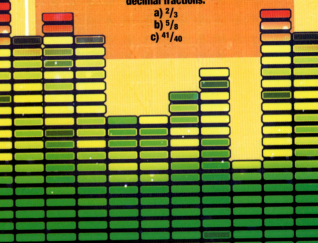

A NEVER-ENDING NUMBER

Pi (also written as π) is one of the most important numbers in maths. It is defined as the circumference of a circle divided by its diameter, and it has the same value regardless of the size of the circle. Pi is an irrational number, meaning that we cannot write down its exact value.

diameter (d)

circumference (c)

pi = c / d

Archimedes (c.287–c.212 BCE)

Greek mathematician and engineer Archimedes was considered the greatest mathematician in the ancient world. He worked out an ingenious way to approximate the value of pi. Archimedes thought about many other mathematical problems. He tried to work out the number of grains of sand that would be needed to fill the universe. To do this, he invented a number system based on the myriad (10,000). He estimated a figure equivalent to 8×10^{63} (8 with 63 zeros after it). Today, we think that the number probably needs 94 zeros!

Approximating pi

Archimedes approximated pi using geometry. He worked out the range between which pi must fall by calculating the lengths of the perimeters of one hexagon (a six-sided polygon) that fitted inside a circle and another that fitted outside it. He then doubled the number of sides of the polygons to 12, 24, 48, and finally 96, which looks almost like a circle. The greater the number of sides, the narrower the range. Using 96-sided polygons, Archimedes calculated that pi must fall between $^{223}/_{71}$ and $^{22}/_{7}$ (3.1408 and 3.1429). He was correct: pi = 3.1416 to four decimal places.

6-sided polygon

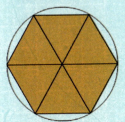 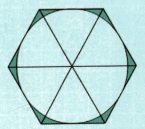

Inner perimeter = 3.0   Outer perimeter = 3.4641

96-sided polygon

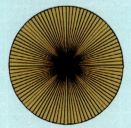 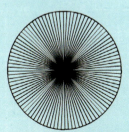

Inner perimeter = 3.1408   Outer perimeter = 3.1429

Pi in the sky

Scientists use pi in lots of their calculations. It is needed in formulas to calculate many different quantities, including the area of a circle (πr^2), the surface area of a sphere ($4\pi r^2$), and the volume of a sphere ($4\pi r^3/3$). Space scientists at NASA used pi to calculate the surface area of Jupiter's moon Europa, which they think may contain life.

Europa is a sphere with a radius of 1,560 km. Using the formula $4\pi r^2$, you can calculate that its surface area is 30 million km^2.

Pi is also needed to calculate the distances between stars, using a maths technique called spherical trigonometry. Scientists need an accurate approximation of pi for these calculations. Modern computers have calculated pi to an accuracy of 22,459,157,718,361 decimal places! To the first 20 decimal places, it looks like this:

π = 3.14159265358979323846

PROJECT: MAKING PI

Approximate the value of pi for yourself.

You will need: a piece of card, a compass and pencil, a protractor, a ruler, a pair of scissors, glue and paper

1. Draw a circle on the card and use the protractor to divide it into 12 equal sectors. The angle of each sector should equal 30° (360° ÷ 12).
2. Divide one of the sectors into two equal sectors with a 15° angle. Number the sectors from 1 to 13.
3. Cut out the 13 sectors and rearrange them so that they roughly form a rectangle.
4. The height of the rectangle is the circle's radius. Its width is half of the curved parts of the sectors, in other words half the circumference.

We know that the circumference $c = 2\pi r$, so the width of the rectangle must equal πr. Divide the width of the rectangle by the height to give an approximation of π.

To give a more accurate approximation, you can use a bigger circle or divide it into more sectors. For instance, you could divide it into 25 sectors (23 with angle 15° and 2 with angle 7.5°).

THE FIBONACCI SEQUENCE

The Fibonacci sequence is a series of numbers produced by adding the two previous numbers in the sequence together. The sequence crops up in many unexpected places.

Leonardo Fibonacci (1175–1250)

The Fibonacci sequence is named after the Italian mathematician Leonardo Fibonacci. He was the son of a wealthy merchant and, as a child, he travelled with his father, meeting people from around the world. He would ask how they did their arithmetic and discovered the Hindu-Arabic number system, using the digits 0–9, that we all use today. Fibonacci popularised this system in his book *Liber Abaci* (*The Book of Calculation*), which also included a description of the Fibonacci sequence.

Breeding rabbits

Fibonacci posed the following problem: At the start of a year, Fibonacci is given a pair of new-born rabbits, one male and one female. After one month, the pair mate, and a month after that, the female gives birth to another pair, one male, one female. If all the females mate immediately after giving birth, and all the rabbits survive, how many pairs of rabbits will Fibonacci have after one year?

The answer was the Fibonacci sequence. Each month, you have all the pairs that were alive last month, plus each pair that was alive the month before that has produced a new pair, so the total each month is the sum of the previous two months. Normally written with a zero at the front, the Fibonacci sequence looks like this:

0 1 1 2 3 5 8 13 21 34 55 89 144 233

At the end of the year, Fibonacci will have 233 rabbits. Like the populations of rabbits, the numbers in the Fibonacci sequence get big very quickly.

Golden spiral

The Fibonacci sequence can be used to create a shape called a golden spiral. The spiral is made by drawing arcs inside squares with sides the length of a Fibonacci number. The golden spiral is an example of a logarithmic spiral. Logarithmic spirals are found in many places in nature. The shells of molluscs such as the nautilis grow in a logarithmic spiral that is close to the golden spiral. The spiral allows them to grow larger without changing shape.

The shell of the nautilis grows in the form of a logarithmic spiral.

13

3

2

1

21

5

8

PROJECT:
FINDING FIBONACCI

Fibonacci numbers are found in the arrangements of seeds and flower heads. Can you find any in your garden?

You will need: pad and pen

The seed head of a sunflower will often have 55 or 89 spirals. The number of petals on a flower is also often a Fibonacci number. Count the seed spirals or petals on a variety of flowers.

Which Fibonacci numbers can you find?

55th spiral

1st spiral

PASCAL'S TRIANGLE

Pascal's triangle is an arrangement of numbers made using a very simple rule. It has an amazing array of properties.

Blaise Pascal (1623–1662)

French scientist Blaise Pascal made many contributions to the fields of mathematics and physics. In 1653, Pascal was the first person to describe many of the properties of the triangle that is now named after him, which he called 'the arithmetical triangle'.

The first eight rows of the triangle

- All 1's
- Counting numbers
- Triangular numbers
- Tetrahedral numbers
- Pentelope numbers

Normal distribution

The numbers in each row of a Pascal's triangle produce a graph called the normal distribution. The normal distribution is found in many areas of statistics, such as average heights of people, average scores in tests or average errors in measurements.

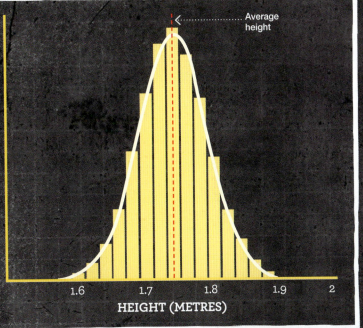

In a normal distribution such as this one plotting the heights of a group of adults, most values are found near the average.

To make a Pascal's triangle, first you make a triangle starting at the top with one cell. Each row has one more cell in it than the row above it. The number in each cell is the sum of the two numbers directly above it. This simple formula creates a pattern with many different properties.

1. The first diagonal is all 1s.

2. The second diagonal is the counting numbers (whole numbers without zero): 1, 2, 3, 4, 5, 6, 7, etc.

3. The third diagonal gives the triangular numbers, which is the number of dots that can be arranged to form a triangle:

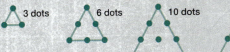

3 dots   6 dots   10 dots   15 dots

4. The fourth diagonal is the tetrahedral numbers. This is the number of spheres that you can form into a tetrahedron, which is a regular four-sided shape.

4 spheres   10 spheres

The sum of each row is twice the previous row: **1, 2, 4, 8, 16, 32, 64, 128**. These can also be written as powers of two: $2^0, 2^1, 2^2, 2^3, 2^4, 2^5, 2^6, 2^7$

PROJECT: DROPPING MARBLES

A quincunx board has pegs arranged as a Pascal's triangle, through which marbles are dropped. Dropped from the top, a marble has an equal chance of falling left or right on each peg. Counting the number of marbles that fall through each gap at the bottom gives a normal distribution. With the help of an adult, you can build your own quincunx by fixing nails to a piece of plywood. Alternatively, there are virtual quincunxes on the Internet, such as here: https://www.mathsisfun.com/data/quincunx.html

1. The sum of the seventh row of a Pascal's triangle is 64. Dropping the marble 64 times down the quincunx three times produced these distributions:
1 10 17 18 12 6 0
1 7 15 14 17 10 1
0 7 10 26 15 6 0
which compare to the sixth line of the Pascal's triangle:
1 6 15 20 15 6 1

Each time you test the quincunx, it will give a slightly different answer, but the average over an infinite number of goes will be the numbers on a Pascal's triangle.

DRAWING GRAPHS

Cartesian coordinates mark a point on a graph by how far long on the *x*-axis and how far up on the *y*-axis it is. As *x* increases, the point moves further right. As *y* increases, the point moves up.

René Descartes (1596–1950)

Cartesian coordinates are named after the French philosopher and mathematician René Descartes. He invented the *x*,*y* coordinate system to study geometry. This allowed him to describe the shapes on a graph in the form of algebraic equations.

The results of equations can be plotted (drawn) next to one another on a graph.

Equations in which *y* is a multiple of *x* create straight lines on a graph.

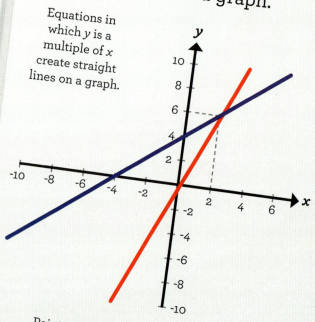

Points at which lines intersect give the values of *x* for which the value of *y* is the same for both equations.

$y = 3x$ $y = x + 4$

These two lines intersect at $x = 2$, $y = 6$

Three-dimensional graphs

Cartesian graphs can also plot the values of three values: x, y and z. Each axis is at right angles to both of the others, meaning that this kind of graph can be used to plot the position of a point in three dimensions.

The three directions of space are each represented by one axis. Three numbers are needed to specify position: one number for each axis.

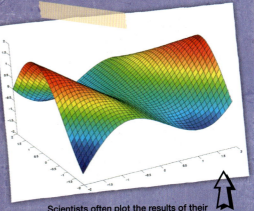

Scientists often plot the results of their research using three-dimensional graphs plotted on computers.

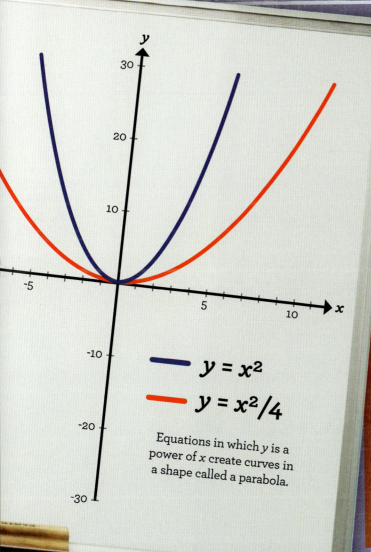

$$y = x^2$$

$$y = x^2/4$$

Equations in which y is a power of x create curves in a shape called a parabola.

PROJECT: TREASURE HUNT

You are on the hunt for a long-lost pirate's treasure. On the wreck of the pirate's ship you find a map of the island where the treasure is buried, along with three gold coins giving different coordinates. Only one of the coins leads to the treasure. The other two coins lead to booby traps set for the unwary treasure hunter. The pirate has written a riddle underneath his map. Can you solve the riddle?

You will need: your feet, your wits

To find my treasure, start at this useless wreck (5, 2) and take two paces along the shore. Take twice as many paces away from the sea, and my gold will be yours. Tread carefully, for dangers lie hidden.

Which coin should you follow to find your treasure? Put a ruler across the line from the wreck to the treasure. Can you find the equation that this line represents?

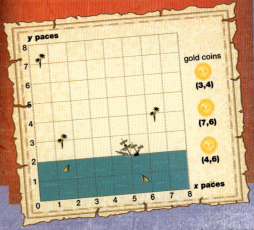

y paces

gold coins

(3,4)

(7,6)

(4,6)

x paces

A CALCULATING MACHINE

Computers use mathematics to represent quantities as varied as musical notes or colours. One of the first people to see how this could be done was the 18th-century mathematician Ada Lovelace.

Ada Lovelace (1815–1852)

The daughter of poet Lord Byron, Ada Lovelace described her approach to problems as 'poetical science'. She saw the potential of a computing machine to solve complex problems, and is credited with writing the first ever computer program. She wrote it for a calculating machine called the Analytic Engine, designed but never built by fellow Briton and close friend Charles Babbage (1791–1871).

Babbage's Analytic Engine worked using a series of mechanical gears, and was designed to be programmed using punch cards.

The first computer program

Lovelace's program calculated a set of numbers called the Bernoulli numbers. These are numbers that play an important role in advanced mathematical analysis. As well as performing mathematical calculations, Lovelace saw the potential for computers like the Analytic Engine to be programmed to do many of the tasks that modern computers can perform, such as drawing graphics and playing music. It can do this because there is a mathematical relation between parts of a drawing and notes in a piece of music.

Babbage was unable to build his Analytic Engine, but the Science Museum in London has launched a project to build it based on his original drawings. It will look like the model shown left. If they succeed, they will be able to run Lovelace's program on it.

PROJECT:
CREATING A MUSIC PROGRAM

Use punch cards to make a simple program to play musical chords. These 12 punch cards represent the keys on a piano keyboard over one full octave.

You will need: 12 pieces of card, hole punch

1 = C **2** = C# **3** = D **4** = D# **5** = E **6** = F

7 = F# **8** = G **9** = G# **10** = A **11** = A# **12** = B

To make the chord C major, you need to play the notes C, E and G (in blue), which would correspond to placing the punch cards 1, 5 and 8 together.

Find the right cards for the chords D minor (D, F, A) and E major (E, G#, B). Can you see a problem with this program in making chords for A, B, F and G? How would you solve the problem?

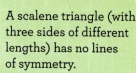

SYMMETRICAL SHAPES

Symmetry is the property of a shape that means it stays the same after it has been flipped or turned.

Reflective symmetry

Reflective symmetry divides a shape such as a triangle into two identical parts along a line called a line of symmetry.

An isosceles triangle (with two sides of equal length) has one line of symmetry.

An equilateral triangle (with all three sides of equal length) has three lines of symmetry.

A scalene triangle (with three sides of different lengths) has no lines of symmetry.

Rotational symmetry

Rotational symmetry is found where a shape stays the same after it has been rotated around a point by an angle other than 360°. Playing cards have rotational symmetry for 180°, meaning that they look the same when rotated half-way. This is known as rotational symmetry order 2.

Playing cards look the same whichever way up you hold them.

Emmy Noether (1882–1935)

One of the most brilliant mathematicians of the 20th century, German Emmy Noether was denied a job in a university because women were barred from holding such positions at the time. Despite this, Noether made important contributions to many fields of mathematics. She used the mathematics of symmetry to demonstrate why physical properties such as energy or momentum are conserved (the total stays the same). Her work explains many of the basic principles of physics. Among many other things, it shows how the symmetrical shape of a bicycle's wheels allows its angular momentum to be conserved: put simply, we don't fall off our bicycles due to the power of symmetry!

Rotational symmetry order 3

This three-legged man appears on the flag of the Isle of Man. It has rotational symmetry for 120°, meaning that it stays the same when rotated by one third of a full circle around its centre. This is rotational symmetry order 3.

PROJECT: SYMMETRICAL FLAGS

Many national flags have symmetrical shapes. Look at these three flags below (1. Switzerland, 2. South Africa, 3. USA), and answer the following questions.

1. Which flag has just one line of reflective symmetry?
2. Which flag has no lines of reflective symmetry?
3. Which flag has rotational symmetry, and which order is it? How many lines of reflective symmetry does this flag have?

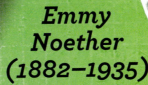

Take a look at other national flags and describe their symmetry.

Is your national flag symmetrical?

We count using the decimal number system, also known as base 10 – a digit for each finger or thumb on our hands. With no hands to count on, just switches that can be either on or off, computers only recognise two digits: 0 or 1. Computers count in a number system known as base 2, or binary.

Decimal to binary

In base 10 (decimal), each digit represents a power of 10: 1, 10, 100, etc. For example, the number 22 represents the following:

1,000s	100s	10s	1s
0	0	2	2
0 +	0 +	2 +	2 = 22

In base 2, each digit represents a power of 2: 1, 2, 4, 8, 16, etc. So the decimal number 22 is represented by the five-digit binary number 10110, as follows:

16s	8s	4s	2s	1s
1	0	1	1	0
16 +	0 +	4 +	2 +	0 = 22

Here are the decimal numbers 1–9 in binary:

1 = 0001	4 = 0100	7 = 0111
2 = 0010	5 = 0101	8 = 1000
3 = 0011	6 = 0110	9 = 1001

Alan Turing (1912–1954)

In the 1930s, British mathematician Alan Turing showed how computers could solve problems by counting in binary. Particularly gifted at logic problems, Turing later led a team of code-breakers during the Second World War. He designed a system that broke the code of the Enigma machine, which was used by the German navy to send secret messages.

Turing machine

In 1936, Turing described a machine that could solve any problem that a modern computer can solve. The machine consists of an infinitely long tape divided into squares. Each square can have either a 0 or a 1 on it. The machine has a head that is positioned over one of the squares on the tape. The head has its own tape of zeros and ones giving it instructions, and it performs the following operation:

1. It reads the number on the square and records it.
2. It either changes the number on the square or leaves the number as it is.
3. It moves the tape by one square either left or right or, if the solution has been found, it stops.

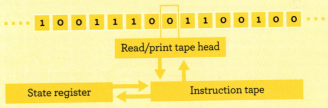

Turing showed that, with enough tape, any computing problem could be solved on his imaginary machine. By doing this, he provided the mathematical model for modern computing, in which programs perform computations using just zeros and ones.

PROJECT:
WRITE YOUR NAME IN BINARY

Each number in a computer's memory is called a bit. To code for a letter in the alphabet requires a total of five digits, or bits. Here are the letters A to Z in five-bit binary code.

You will need: a pen, piece of paper

A 00001	**G** 00111	**M** 01101	**S** 10011	**Y** 11001
B 00010	**H** 01000	**N** 01110	**T** 10100	**Z** 11010
C 00011	**I** 01001	**O** 01111	**U** 10101	
D 00100	**J** 01010	**P** 10000	**V** 10110	
E 00101	**K** 01011	**Q** 10001	**W** 10111	
F 00110	**L** 01100	**R** 10010	**X** 11000	

Can you write out your name in binary code? This code only has upper-case letters. To make a binary code with both upper-case letters and lower-case letters for the whole alphabet, how many bits would you need?

MAKING A DECISION

Game theory is the study of how and why people make decisions. Game theorists create mathematical formulas to assess situations in which one person's decisions affect the results of decisions made by other people. Game theory helps businesses to make investment choices and scientists to model the process of evolution.

John Nash (1928–2015)

In 1950, American student John Nash wrote his PhD thesis on game theory. Nash defined a solution to games now called the Nash equilibrium. This is the situation in which a player of a game is making the best decision they can given their knowledge of the other players. A brilliant mathematician with mental health problems, Nash's troubled life was portrayed in the film *A Beautiful Mind*.

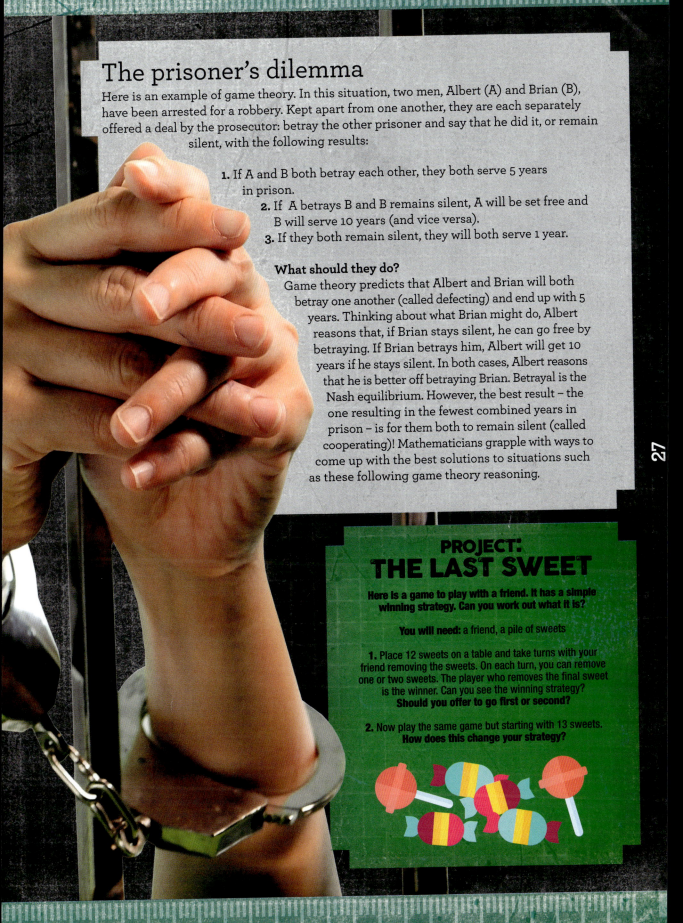

The prisoner's dilemma

Here is an example of game theory. In this situation, two men, Albert (A) and Brian (B), have been arrested for a robbery. Kept apart from one another, they are each separately offered a deal by the prosecutor: betray the other prisoner and say that he did it, or remain silent, with the following results:

1. If A and B both betray each other, they both serve 5 years in prison.
2. If A betrays B and B remains silent, A will be set free and B will serve 10 years (and vice versa).
3. If they both remain silent, they will both serve 1 year.

What should they do?

Game theory predicts that Albert and Brian will both betray one another (called defecting) and end up with 5 years. Thinking about what Brian might do, Albert reasons that, if Brian stays silent, he can go free by betraying. If Brian betrays him, Albert will get 10 years if he stays silent. In both cases, Albert reasons that he is better off betraying Brian. Betrayal is the Nash equilibrium. However, the best result – the one resulting in the fewest combined years in prison – is for them both to remain silent (called cooperating)! Mathematicians grapple with ways to come up with the best solutions to situations such as these following game theory reasoning.

PROJECT:
THE LAST SWEET

Here is a game to play with a friend. It has a simple winning strategy. Can you work out what it is?

You will need: a friend, a pile of sweets

1. Place 12 sweets on a table and take turns with your friend removing the sweets. On each turn, you can remove one or two sweets. The player who removes the final sweet is the winner. Can you see the winning strategy? **Should you offer to go first or second?**

2. Now play the same game but starting with 13 sweets. **How does this change your strategy?**

FRACTAL GEOMETRY

The shapes found in nature may look chaotic, but many of them can be created by repeating a few very simple mathematical rules. Known as fractals, these shapes have a property called self-similarity, meaning that they look much the same close up as they do from far away.

Benoit Mandelbrot (1924–2010)

French-American Benoit Mandelbrot was one of the first mathematicians to use computers to draw fractal shapes. He discovered a fractal now known as the Mandelbrot set that uses a simple formula to create an extraordinary amount of complexity and beauty when its results are drawn by a computer.

As you zoom in on the edge of the Mandelbrot set (the whole set is shown top left), coiled 'seahorse' shapes appear. Zooming in even further, shapes similar to the whole set appear.

⊛ Fractals in nature

Clouds are an example of fractals in nature. Their self-similarity makes it very hard to tell exactly how far away they are.

Trees have a fractal shape. Following simple mathematical rules, the central trunk divides into smaller and smaller branches, ending in narrow twigs.

Sierpinski triangle

The Sierpinski triangle is a fractal shape made by dividing an equilateral triangle into four smaller triangles, removing the middle one, then repeating this step on each triangle. This simple pattern has been used to decorate churches and mosques for many centuries.

PROJECT:
MAKE A KOCH SNOWFLAKE

A Koch snowflake is a fractal made entirely out of triangles. To make one, follow these steps.

You will need: a ruler, piece of paper, a pen

1. Draw a large equilateral triangle.
2. Divide each side into thirds.
3. Draw an equilateral triangle on each middle third.
4. Divide each outer side of these three triangles into thirds and draw a triangle on each middle third.
5. Repeat as many times as you can.

The Koch snowflake was first described by the mathematician Helge von Koch in 1904. The more triangles you add to it, the longer its perimeter becomes, while its area gets closer and closer to 8/5 times the area of the original triangle, but never quite reaches it. Can you see how many times the pattern to the right has been repeated?

ALGEBRA
A branch of mathematics that uses letters to represent unknown numbers in equations or formulas.

ANGULAR MOMENTUM
A measure of the rotation of an object such as a spinning wheel.

ARITHMETIC
The branch of mathematics that involves adding, multiplying, subtracting or dividing numbers.

AXIOM
A statement in mathematics that is accepted as true.

BASE
The number of digits used to represent numbers in a counting system.

DECIMAL PLACE
The position of a digit to the right of a decimal point.

DIMENSION
A measurement in a particular direction. Three dimensions are needed to define a position in space.

EQUILATERAL TRIANGLE
A triangle with three angles of 60° and three sides of equal length.

GEOMETRY
The branch of mathematics that deals with space and shapes.

PERIMETER
The continuous line forming the border of a geometric shape.

POLYGON
A two-dimensional shape formed from three or more straight lines.

POWER
The power of a number tells you how many times to multiply the number by itself.

SET
A collection of objects or numbers with a certain quality in common.

THEOREM
A statement in mathematics that has been proved to be true.

VARIABLE
A number whose value is unknown.

p.11 Decimal fractions

a) 0.666...   b) 0.625   c) 1.025

p.19 Treasure hunt

The treasure is found at the location indicated by the coin marked (7, 6). Moving in the other direction will take you to location (3, 6), which is not shown by a coin.

A line from the wreck to the treasure passes through (5, 2) and (7, 6). This represents the equation $y = 2x - 8$.

p.15 Finding Fibonacci

Examples of Fibonacci numbers you may have found include:

Lily: 3 petals, Buttercup: 3 petals, Ragwort: 13 petals, Daisy: 34 or 55 petals

Some plants may not have exactly a Fibonacci number. Some petals may have fallen off or may not have grown yet.

p.21 Creating a music program

D minor: 3, 6 and 10   E major: 5, 9, 12

To make chords for F, G, A and B, you need to add keys for a higher octave. To program for this, you could add a 13th hole with one more punch card that will cover that hole to indicate that the note is the higher octave.

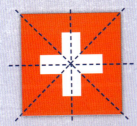

p.23 Symmetrical flag

The flag of South Africa has just one line of reflective symmetry. The flag of the USA has no lines of symmetry. The flag of Switzerland has rotational symmetry order 4. It also has four lines of reflective symmetry.

p.25 Write your name in binary

There are 52 letters altogether, so you need six bits (digits) to write them all out (52 in base 10 is 110100 in base 2). Six bits gives you a total of 64 (2^6) different combinations, so you will have 12 bits spare to code for other things.

p.27 The last sweet

You need to avoid having to move at any point where there are multiples of 3 sweets on the table: 3, 6, 9, 12, etc. As soon as your opponent has a multiple of 3 sweets on their turn, you know you can win: if they remove 1, you take 2; if they remove 2, you take 1. This leaves them with another multiple of 3 until their final turn with 3 sweets left, when they cannot stop you from winning next go. So with 12 sweets on the table, you need to go second. With 13 sweets, offer to take the first go, and take one sweet.

p.29 Make a Koch snowflake

The pattern has been repeated 6 times on this Koch snowflake.

INDEX